BUG JOKES

Compiled by Pam Rosenberg
Illustrated by Patrick Girouard

Special thanks to Donna Hynek and her second grade class of 2005–2006 for sharing their favorite jokes.

Published in the United States of America by The Child's World®
PO Box 326, Chanhassen, MN 55317-0326
800-599-READ
www.childsworld.com

Acknowledgments
    The Child's World®: Mary Berendes, Publishing Director

    Editorial Directions, Inc.: E. Russell Primm, Editorial Director and Line
    Editor; Katie Marsico, Managing Editor; Assistant Editor, Caroline Wood;
    Susan Ashley, Proofreader

    The Design Lab: Kathleen Petelinsek, Designer; Kari Tobin,
    Page Production

Library of Congress Cataloging-in-Publication Data
    Bug jokes / compiled by Pam Rosenberg; illustrated by Patrick Girouard.
        p. cm. — (Laughing matters)
    ISBN-13: 978-1-59296-706-3
    ISBN-10: 1-59296-706-X (library bound: alk. paper)
    1. Insects—Juvenile humor. I. Rosenberg, Pam. II. Girouard, Patrick.
III. Title. IV. Series.
    PN6231.I56B84 2007
    818'.60208036257—dc22   2006022652

BEES

Why do bees hum?
Because they don't know the words.

How do bees comb their hair?
With a honeycomb.

What do bees wear to school?
Yellow jackets.

What kind of animal says zzub?
A bee flying backwards.

What do you call a young bee?
A babe-bee.

What is a bee's favorite song?
"Stingin' in the Rain"

6

What do bees chew?
Bumblegum.

What did the farmer get when he tried to call the beehive?
A buzzy signal.

What kind of bee lives in a graveyard?
A zombee.

What goes "hum-choo, hum-choo"?
A bee with a cold.

How did the bumblebee get to school?
He rode the school buzz.

What would you get if you crossed a parrot and a bumblebee? An animal that talks all the time about how busy it is.

What did the bee say to the flower? Hey, Bud, when do you open?

What kind of bee drops its honey? A spilling bee.

What do bees wear to the beach? Bee-kinis.

Where do bees go if they want to take public transportation? To the buzz stop.

What kind of weapon goes "buzz, buzz"
when you pull the trigger?
   A bee-bee gun.

Where does a bee sit?
   On his bee-hind.

What did the bee say to the flower?
   Hello, Honey!

What does a bee order at McDonald's?
   A humburger.

What did one bee say to the other bee
during the summer?
   Swarm in here, isn't it?

Who is a bee's favorite classical music composer?
Bee-thoven.

Why do bees buzz?
Because they don't know how to whistle.

How many bees were in the bee choir?
A humdred.

What do you get if you cross a bee with a doorbell?
A hum dinger.

What do you call a bee born in May?
A maybe.

BUTTERFLIES & MOTHS

What do insects learn at school?
Mothmatics.

What's green and dangerous?
A caterpillar with a bad temper.

What's the biggest moth in the world?
The mammoth.

Anna: Why is there a moth in my soup?
School Cook: The fly must be on vacation!

Why did the caterpillar go to the library?
He wanted to be a bookworm.

Why couldn't the butterfly go to the dance?
Because it was a moth ball.

Why was the little insect crying?
It wanted its moth-er.

What do you get when you eat caterpillars?
Butterflies in your stomach.

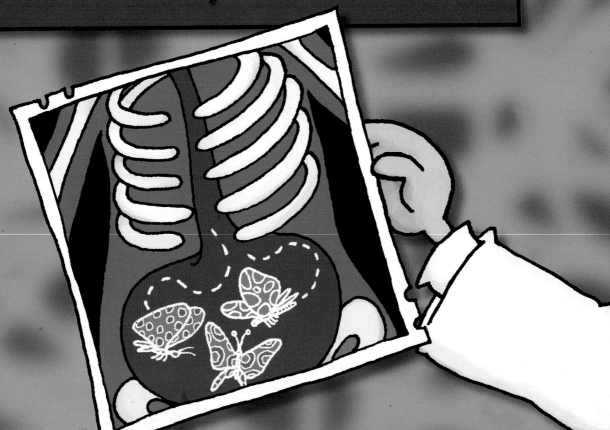

FLEAS

What did one flea say to the other after a night out?
Shall we walk home or take a dog?

What's the difference between a flea and a wolf?
One prowls on the hairy and the other howls on the prairie.

What do you get if you cross a rabbit and a flea?
Bugs Bunny.

Who can leap tall poodles in a single bound?
Super Flea!

What's the best place to buy bugs?
At a flea market.

How do fleas travel?
They itch-hike.

FLIES

Customer: What is this fly doing in my soup?
Waiter: I think he's doing the backstroke.

Diner: Waiter, there's a fly in my soup!
Waiter: Well, keep quiet about it or everyone will want one.

How do you keep flies out of the kitchen?
Put a pile of manure in the living room.

If there are five flies in the kitchen, how do you know which one is a football player?
He's the one in the sugar bowl.

What's the difference between a fly and a bird?
A bird can fly, but a fly can't bird!

What do you call a fly without wings?
A walk.

What has four wheels and flies?
A garbage truck.

Why did the flies go to Paris?
Because they wanted to be French flies.

What has four legs and flies?
A picnic table.

GRASSHOPPERS & CRICKETS

What do you call a bug that jumps over cups?
A glasshopper.

What's green and can jump a mile in a minute?
A grasshopper with hiccups.

What's an insect's favorite game?
Cricket.

MOSQUITOES

What do you get if you cross the Lone Ranger with a mosquito?
The Masked-quito!

When are mosquitoes most annoying?
When they get under your skin.

What has six legs and talks in code?
A Morse-quito.

What do you get when you cross a mosquito with a hippo?
I'm not sure, but if it stings you, you'll be in big trouble!

What did the mosquito say the first time it saw a camel?
Did I do that?

What's a mosquito's favorite sport?
Skin diving.

18

SPIDERS

What's the best kind of computer bug?
Spiders. They make the best Web sites.

Where do spiders go to learn new words?
Web-ster's Dictionary.

Why did the spider cross the information superhighway?
It wanted to get to its Web site.

Diner: Waiter, there's a dead spider in my soup!
Waiter: Yes, sir, they aren't very good swimmers.

What do you call two spiders who just got married?
Newlywebs.

19

MISCELLANEOUS

What do you get if you cross the Beatles with the Rolling Stones?
The Squashed Bugs.

What kind of bugs live in clocks?
Ticks.

How do fireflies start a race?
"Ready, set, glow!"

Why did the insect get kicked out of the park?
He was a litterbug.

What do you call a bug with four wheels and a trunk?
A Volkswagen Beetle.

Where do they take sick insects?
To the wasp-ital.

Who was the greatest insect baseball player?
Mickey Mantis.

What do you say to a smart firefly?
"For a little guy, you're very bright!"

21

Sarah: Mommy, are bugs good to eat?
Mom: I don't think we should talk about bugs at dinner.
Mom (while washing dishes after dinner): Now what is it that you wanted to ask me?
Sarah: Oh, never mind. There was a bug in my stew, but now it's gone!

Patient: Doctor, what is the best way to prevent diseases caused by biting insects?
Doctor: Don't bite any!

What do you get if you cross a bee with a skunk? An animal that stinks and stings.

What is a tick's favorite game? Tic-tac-toe.

What do insects use to write reports? Flypaper.

What does a baby bug ride in? A buggy.

What is a centipede's favorite toy? Leg-os.

Why was the centipede late for school?
    Because he was playing "This Little Piggy" with his baby brother.

How do we know that insects are smart?
    They always know when we're eating outside.

What do you get if you cross a centipede with a chicken?
    Enough drumsticks to feed an army.

What's worse than an alligator with a toothache?
    A centipede with athlete's foot.

A farmer was milking his cow when a bug flew into the barn. The bug circled the farmer's head, then flew into the cow's ear. The farmer didn't think much about it until the bug squirted out into his bucket. It had gone in one ear and out the udder.

23

About Patrick Girouard:

Patrick Girouard has been illustrating books for almost 15 years but still looks remarkably lifelike. He loves reading, movies, coffee, robots, a beautiful red-haired lady named Rita, and especially his sons, Marc and Max. Here's an interesting fact: A dog named Sam lives under his drawing board. You can visit him (Patrick, not Sam) at www.pgirouard.com.

About Pam Rosenberg:

Pam Rosenberg is a former junior high school teacher and corporate trainer. She currently works as an author, editor, and the mother of Sarah and Jake. She took on this project as a service to all her fellow parents of young children. At least now their kids will have lots of jokes to choose from when looking for the one they will tell their parents over and over and over again!